The So-Called Sonnets

Bruce McRae

Silenced Press

First Edition.

ISBN-13: 978-0-9792410-5-5
ISBN-10: 0-9792410-5-7

Library of Congress Control Number: †

Cover art by Laurie Lipton (www.laurielipton.com)
Cover graphic design by Bill Reed

More information available at:
www.silencedpress.com

The So-Called Contents

Fragile

The quiet, being taken apart
for easy handling and shipping,
the movers tip-toeing, their breaths
measured, working swiftly, yet
cautious. The quiet being sent
away, moved to another part of
town, in sound-proofed boxes, in
padded crates, in rubber cartons
marked 'Handle With Care'. You
can almost hear it, the way its
weight shifts, the dust being
disturbed, the absurd lengths
that the movers go to not to say
a word, their dark eyes rolling.

Painting

Of a river, which is riverish
or riverlike, if not riverine.
Which is a copy of a copy.
A painting on a wall
with a painting of a wall in it.
And the rain with teeth in it,
with a few deft strokes a rain implied.
Art crime, deliriously uninventive,
that I bought in Hyde Park yesterday,
foole upon foole that I am.
With its few representational smears;
that are people, that are peoplesque.
Their faces blobs, like gobbets of drool,
or flecks of redoubtable snot.

Intolerable Mirage

A morning so heavy that light
cannot escape its surface. A
moving cloud of barely visible
excitement crossing a frost-burnt
field as if to get a last word in,
a sort of ism, the messenger and
message in one, an irrational
phenomenon of largely indifferent
anomalous forces trying to hitch
a ghost ride back into Darktown.
A random thing lurching our
way, proffering us its poppies.
And some birds too, somewhat bored
with this, their laughs infectious.

Eternal Flame

The night the house of love burnt
down. The night the eminent shrink
informed us: Sometimes, a cigar is
just a cigar, but his erection more than
obvious, the Bluestockings in hushed
awe, some of them quietly reaching for
their tissues. "What do women want?"
the world-renowned psycho-analyst asks
as he fumbles for his matches on the dais,
an elderly matron first crossing and then
uncrossing her legs. A poem in which alarm
bells are going off all over town, firemen
throwing their trousers on, fire engines
entering the first of the long dark tunnels.

Flag

It's nights like this I ask myself,
what is a flag? A fluttering
symbol of a nation's amplified
psychosis. A blood-drenched rag
dipped at the passing catafalque.
A handkerchief to wave at the
soldiers marching off to war,
marching against human failure.

Run it up the pole and see who
salutes it. Use it for swaddling,
a bandage after an accident, to
mop the feverish brow of one
unwell. A thing to dry your hands
on after throwing in the towel.

Necktie

It's a ring you climb in and out of
in a futile effort to master chaos.
No, says I, it's a dog's collar and leash
misrepresenting the senescent penis.
You're wrong, it's a silk noose, its knot
mocking the cheap clip-on variety.
Perhaps, I replied, or it's a thumbnail
being dragged across the throat slowly,
a space-time portal where only the head fits
through, a snare for the occasional rabbit.
You'd be right if you weren't so wrong.
It's really a border crossing, a filthy lasso,
the tattoo of a dashed line and tiny scissors
with the words 'Cut here' along it.

Another Story For Another Time

Prince Pedro of Castile was found
sleeping it off in his car. "I've been
thinking of a bridge," he said, "of a
rainbow between two sighs." Oh you
should have seen him, hair uncombed
beneath a crown askew, sitting up in
the back seat, grinning like a schoolboy.
"A few cheerful chirrups wouldn't
go amiss," he cried out at the birds.
Poor poor prince, how his world had
changed since Wednesday. "I'm like
Attila and I screw with words," he
said between slugs from his hip-flask,
the letter in his pocket unopened, unread

A Clock, Ticking

I thought it was a faucet dripping,
the tap-tap-tapping of a blind man's cane.
I thought it was a tiny hammer in a tinier fist,
one usually found pounding on a lectern.
Like those little footsteps, gallows-bound,
each second an egg being cracked open,
each second a fissure in time and space —
big enough to drive a Mack truck through.
It reminds me of my favorite aunt,
knitting needles clicking in another room,
she tut-tutting over my latest indiscretion.
Or it's the smallest of beating horse-hearts.
The eternal breaking of the backs of fleas
between the fingernails of beauty.

Appointed Rounds

The last postman on Earth,
en route in the City of Serpents,
the balance of his mind disturbed,
the mail sack getting lighter and lighter.
And his breaths shorter.

The one bitten by the black dog.
The one with a dead letter,
a trail of rubber bands and twine
leading to Mrs. Lundquist's house,
her front gate squeaking.

The last letter in the world,
but the address smeared in the rain,
in the sleet, in the dark of night.
Which arrived sooner than expected.

Unfounded

It's out there on the same plane
as lost luggage or stardust.
A vanished sock or number
carried off in last month's flood.
The random calculus of mobs.
The jaguar's teeth in mire.
The buried scent under the sawgrass.

It's here too, in a corner of a round room.
It was just here, and now it's somewhere else,
a thing that's not worth mentioning.
A thing gone down a drain
only to rise out of the cold lake,
reaching up like a hand,
missing a ring, missing a finger.

Raise Your Hand

Found. Found. Found.
Under a fingernail once attached
to young Master Aldous Huxley.
Found, as if bedraggled refugees,
scurrying over a dirtied mound of Venus,
blood flowing freely like a fountain
from the Old Rome of a wrist.
Found. At the base of Velikovsky's thumb,
climbing a knuckle for a better view.
Found. Encircling Christ's pinkie.
Leaping from the ring finger to index —
then caught hopping back again. Found
upon the very tip of Aristotle's digitus
impudicus. Poised, accusing, pointing.

Old Glove

The old glove seems miserable, pining for its mate.
The old glove is a thrown tantrum, flung to the floor,
crawling to the farthest corner of a walk-in closet,
that place odd socks and dust-bunnies go when they die.
The old glove's looking more like an old balloon
with the wind knocked out of it, and feeling perfectly useless.
You think it might have sighed, but it's only shivering.
You think of the spider on the cellar's beam,
boney and brittle, its parched innards sucked dry.
The old glove clenches, unclenches, fighting for breath,
gravity winning the struggle, two falls out of three,
tossed down like a defiant gauntlet, for what seemed
a good reason at the time, then hanging on for dear life,
waving goodbye, making a fist of it, cursing the hand.

Newborn

Unfortunate child. Born so ugly
the stars crawled away to die.
So ugly the father scooped
out his eyes with a sugar spoon
and the mother changed sex.
A child so ugly the doctor
gnawed off his hands at the wrist
and animals de-boned themselves.
So ugly, in fact, the seas boiled
and mountains slid under the soil.
The sky fell down and angels went bad.
Sweet, innocent, harmless child . . .
Even Satan's skin crawled.
Even God looked away, downhearted.

All-Inclusive

A club so exclusive that no one
belongs to it. A club so exclusive
that none are allowed to admit to
belonging to it. So exclusive in fact
that nobody knows it exists and
no one is encouraged to join. None
of its non-members are known to
us. Such is its exclusivity that even
those of the shadowy realms doubt
its existence. A club so discreet the
very mention of it has put myself
and my loved ones in great danger.
Listen, you didn't hear this from me,
do you understand? You didn't . . .

Wink

Was it the mote in God's eye?
An errant spark or eyelash?
Is wink the root of 'twinkle'?

That look on Daddy saying,
'you're a mighty fine girl'.
The sly rebus of I.C.U.
The coded quick nudge between us;
hale and hearty co-conspirators
unseen by the spy of patsy.
The wink says 'you're in on it',
'you know what I mean', 'it's time'.

Or is it only half a blink,
Horus's other, lazier, eye to follow,
his watery shorthand for infection?

Zen Advertising Co.

You must be tough yet pliable, such as these radial tires on special offer. You will be soft yet purposeful, that is the strength of our paper tissues now available. It is best to bend, but never to break, in the wind, to snap back into place unhindered for this limited time only. There is no magic pill without a voice within disclaiming its many side effects. If a billboard falls in the storm, will any have read of the benefits our beauty cream promises? What can we know, ever truly know? Faith in yourself, as well as this insurance plan, is all the Cosmos asks of you. What you purchase is the illusion of happiness. The wise man possesses nothing, and gives his money where it is needed most. There is no customer or sale, my friends. There is no product.

Allotment

Put down that book of beautiful gardens
where you can imagine nymphs and water features —
the Bible never said that Eden was destroyed.
Even though the First Couple, and as naked as sin,
were thrown out on their asses for sheer cheek,
Our Lord the Fond Abuser couldn't bring Himself
around to the idea of fallowing His cabbage patch;
one so lovingly cultivated and promising.
In that other placeless dimension
it still blossoms and blooms, a little overgrown,
a little rough around the hedges, but green
and growing, with other even more absurd animals
rooting through the mulch, scratching their heads,
believing themselves the fruit of creation.

His Early Promise Unfulfilled

God spat an ocean, shat the Alps,
pissed torrents and waterfalls.
God wasn't beautiful and frightened
the curly-headed kiddies and nuns.
God drove by in a beat-up rust-bucket,
whistling and shouting and waving a gun.
God played the spoons and bummed quarters
by the entrance to the liquor store.
He planted time bombs in the hearts and minds
of orthodontists and city officials.
What a character! A right barrel of laughs.
Like the time he threw up all over Jupiter.
And the practical jokes; you've seen his platypus.
And the plagues of his miserable temper.

In Purgatory

Limbo, where queues reach toward
the infinite to form a mathematical
construct of hypothetical proportions.
The restless dead, awaiting judgment,
fidgeting impatiently as eternity
unfolds gradually, their expressions
strained, their gazes locked onto
the Great Beyond, emotionless, yet
somehow familiar. As if they'd met
each other many times on a street
in the corporeal plane or had perished
arm in arm. Faces frozen at the hour
of death. An incomprehensible death,
which too unfolded, very slowly.

The Living Hell Bemusement Park

As it turns out, Hell isn't so bad after all:
An air-conditioner humming a little too loudly,
a tap that's dripping constantly,
an iron gate creaking in a summer's breeze,
back and forth, squeaking back and forth . . .
Sinners can come to expect poor television reception,
music not to their particular tastes playing
on every station on a hellish radio, a phone
that rings and rings at every inopportune moment,
the mother-in-law who pops in to visit
unexpectedly then doesn't leave for eons.
The worst bits are a nagging suspicion there's
something important you should have done,
and the eternal roach in the infernal kitchen.

The Temple Of Eviction

Louis, the Stammerer, a puny
phallopath and sensualist, the
shark perfectly at ease among
these blackened waters, lectures,
eventually, on the indeterminacy
of art, the legacy of the Moors, on
Bacchanalia's ugly little step-sister,
Violence, seen first hand, stutters,
"Defilement, defecation, damnation,
require no further explanation."
Saint Louis, the light is breaking
like a bone, the stars our light
we travel by. "And if not the stars,"
he mutters, by and by, "the s-s-sun."

All Hips And Lips And Elbows

They're at it like knives.
He with a full head of steam,
hammer and tongs, like the clappers.
She as if a hot bath,
to be entered slowly,
her country a madness
of implacable being.

The broody musings of mood-music
and the scene is set; a lady's
garden, fields of lady bedstraw
and knotweed. (Look and learn,
little flower, look and learn.)
A bottle and a cigarette.
A whistle and a kiss.

Or Maybe It Was Just Me

We wore each other thin,
a slow grinding, like corn or teeth.
We visited the seaside,
its littoral rank a suspected balm,
the sea a broken mirror,
the sea an unmade bed,
the sea a blood oath left unsaid.
And the ocean wasn't big enough.

Our time passed like a marching band.
We took to the air, like chickens,
the two of us grown smaller,
cold Canada coming closer,
the light between us pale as stars,
the sky getting darker and large.

Peep Show

My love is sky-high and cool as the moon is blue.
It presses pills in the all-night pharmacy.
"Lady," it says, "You dropped a scented handkerchief."
Then it blushes like a schoolgirl,
one who yearns to be with an older man,
a schoolgirl caught with her first cigarette,
a tendril of blood running into her shoe.

Little Miss Rumor, and a gang of gossips,
the street-choir singing Love, so true . . .
My love at the spelling bee but mumbling marbles.
My love at the jamboree, with hay in her hair.
My love with the absinthe eyes and afterglow.
We stride out, defiant, from the underworld.
We pour out our honey and ashes.

Belt

A braid of knotted horsehair,
and I waist-deep in my immodesty.
The serpent as Möbius strip,
each new notch another day unfed.
Money for old rope, or a whip
to crack the backs of the Assyrians.
Here, the circle of suspicion.
There, the human equatorial zone.
Or, it's a portable noose, patent pending,
its buckle a handy knuckle-duster.
"Keep your pants on," my mother said,
and how I wish I'd heeded her advice,
my jeans hung down around my knees,
the river waist-high and rising.

Worst-case Scenario

A scrum of trees. Just hanging
around. Thugs on a northern
street corner, real tough nuts
out-wintering winter, the wind
rifling through their pockets, a
toothpick dangling in each slack-
jawed maw carved by a willful
schoolboy. A bunch of hoods. A
collective noun of urban outcasts
with their backs to the errant
wind, of an anxious mind-set, an
all-singing, all-dancing night
moving in for a rumble; language,
it appears, a powerless weapon.

An Empire In Ruins

Into the heart of the fly,
into its knotted soul,
Death's army marching on nails,
a ditch for make-do mortuary,
flames taking root
under a pawnbroker's sign,
the subnormal biting his chain,
lifting his cup of dust
in a bombed-out meat locker,
somewhere a sea coiling
around a hook in a cellar,
the god of flies wing-deep in snow,
snow as black as a miner's lung
and flung from a brain-grey sky.

Jolly Roger

Met a man who found a treasure.
Buried? I asked, not believing him.
Pirates? I asked, disinterested.
No, he didn't say. Or was it yes,
his face unlike the map imagined
handed down through family,
in the lining of a sailor's cap, a drawer,
found with a privateer's mementoes.
Hidden? I asked, becoming curious,
his mouth like an X on an island.
Sunken!? I shouted, demanding to know.
He grinned and crossed his arms,
just so, not unlike a skull and crossbones.
Nothing, he answered, unsmiling.

Chef Recommends The Famine

That's my heart they're serving up
on a plate. And it's medium-rare.
That's my little spunk-rat heart
they're dishing out; delightfully saucy,
basting in its own juices, piping hot.
I'm on the menu; it's a secret family
recipe going back for generations.
"A hint of cloves and a touch of garlic,
that's what the thing tastes of to me,"
that's what the thin girl says to the fat man,
she playing with her food between sighs,
he snapping his fingers at the waiter.
"Garçon! Another bottle of your finest,"
he says, she pushing her dinner aside.

Flyleaf

Everywhere the great poets are dying,
dropping like hints before a birthday,
like the mercury in a Siberian thermometer,
like concrete slabs from a highway overpass;
dropping like trousers at a military medical exam
or names among celebrities.
As if a bar of soap in a prison's showers.
Falling like a meth addict's IQ, or a castle wall.
Like the value of a pre-war mark.
Falling like Fat Boy over Hiroshima.
Like the scented gloves of courtesans.
Everywhere the great poets are falling,
as if a book from a hand to the bedroom floor,
its pages creased, the author sleeping.

Death's Epic

All the murdered poets rising from the seabed,
who stride ashore through the murderous surf,
crowned in kelp, in gowns of whitewater,
'slumbering Thebes' on their kill-cold lisps,
who said dead before all others, then died,
maddened by such minds and pills and firewater,
self-murdered by the very thing, the poetry . . .

Inglorious death by insult to the brain.
Death by ocean-going steamer. Death by bridge.
Death by oven, shotgun, whiskey, love.
A question for these dancers in the sand:
Which came first, the utter madness or the line?
Just one word, just a skeletal hand on a bloodied page.
I saw it was a name like theirs, written over and over.

Pomes

Poem. And to sing is to pray twice.
The unintelligible one has spoken —
poem, like a cold and dirty room,
the brief light low, and yet too bright,
the mask of respectability marred.
Poem, the color of cold tea, like
a walk in the dark, knitted into a
jewel from raggle-taggle threads.
Poem, neutered by failure and age,
small-talk descended from microbes,
revised, like analyzing a troublesome
dream; punchdrunk and wheedling.
Like a rope thrown down to climb.
Like a very determined insect.

I Know Now

The old man was as mad as a box of cats.
He stood eyeball to eyeball with a flowery skunk
without good reason; he drove off to the dump
and shot my dog then claimed he hadn't;
he took up the snake, cracked it like a whip,
he broke its neck, if not a neck, its back,
and threw it like a green stick at the garden.

The snake-eating snake, the desert sidewinder,
king cobra, the black mamba with its neurotoxins
strong enough to clock a horse — none of these,
as I know now, but a harmless refugee from Eden:
He gladly snapped and gave it one good lash.
And once a rabid dog had crossed his path. It didn't
stand a chance, he said, and laughed and laughed.

No Salesmen, No Flyers

"Get that chicken out of here," my
mother readily insisted, refusing
to be lectured on her own doorstep.
We all hid behind the chesterfield
when the proselytes came skulking
around (God bless them all). "Knock
knock," she would say as the milk-
man pulled up at the front of our
house clinking like a good one. "I'm
in the bath," dear mama would yell
from the kitchen, trying to catch our
mailman unaware. Oh, and that poor
chicken; it didn't know which way to
look when the oven door was opened.

Those Weren't The Days

Without a TV we would watch the fire.
Without a radio we'd sing.
Without electricity we'd read by candlelight.
Yes we were poor, but we were happy.

Those were the days: a seven mile
walk to school through snow,
an orange for Christmas,
the four of us tucked into one bed . . .

And we made our own fun then,
sometimes a quiz of made-up questions
or hide 'n' seek around the table.

I was the youngest and Ma called me 'Babe'.
I grew to be the toughest kid
but got the dirtiest bathwater.

Don't Kid Yourself

In the School of the Bloody Obvious
small kindnesses go unrewarded.
If you stand up too suddenly waves
of vertigo and nausea overcome
even the most hardy of students.
Lessons are samey and all-inclusive.
Behind the bike shed you'll find a lot
of smoking going on, much as expected.
Opiates, neuropathogens and psychotropics
aggravate your classmates' narcolepsy.
The sense of reproach is almost tangible.
Praise is showered only on the fortunate.
What goes up, you may have already
guessed, always comes down.

The Doctor Is In

The doctor will see you now.
The young intern swinging
his stethoscope in a devil-may-care fashion.
The old surgeon, his cigarette
dangling from a quivering lower lip.
The flimflam MD, his phony doctorate
really a certificate in plumbing.
And kindly Doc Thompson,
who's watched them come and seen them go,
whole generations gone missing.
He's speaking with little Jenny now.
"Am I going to die?" she asks.
"As sure as sugar darling," he says,
"As sure as shooting."

Youth, Like Beauty, Fading

The calm forests and skies' majesties.
These goes unnoticed in McGinty's Bar,
and still an hour until the noon rush.
God moves his hand over the marvelous waters
while the streetsweeper orders a glass of ale,
the old sop at the end of the bar since opening
and he discussing basketball and backsides,
a magnificent light touching the smoke-
stained curtains, a fly buzz-bombing the window.
The blue and green of the world turns
through the vast and velvety cosmic void
as an on-leave sailor lights his cigarette.
The girl behind the bar makes the littlest sigh,
no more than the breath of a swallow.

Dirty Word

A dirty word left Uncle Elmer's mouth.
A nasty little word, not nice at all.
It flew around the house wildly,
ricocheting off the lampshades,
killing the parakeet, tearing mum's new curtains,
leaving a filthy stain on every wall and knick-knack,
scratching paint, even cracking the fishbowl.
The dirty word bit Aunt Gladys on the lip.
It hit Davina in the temple, causing much concern.
My father said, "Elmer."
"Yes Nelson." My father said,
"I wish you wouldn't swear in front of the children."
The kids, meanwhile, were under the house,
playing with matches and porn.

A Bar Of Soap

Soap is the brother to candles.
A little egg, one incapable
of washing its own face.
A whitefish tackling the rapids
of a bubbly hot bath.
A flower behind bars.
A stone skipping over the waves,
worn smooth by gales and rain,
easily squeezed into a ball
or the most personal of crannies.
Slippery devil, the sound of water
running away with the sink.
The sound of the one hand
scrubbing the other.

Serving Writ

They broke my little black heart.
Those mealy-mouthed, sod-minded,
streptococcus-ridden gobdaws.
That wasn't mentioned in the manual
for The Graveyard School of Poetry.
That wasn't covered in the guidebook.

I admit some moral shortcomings,
I might be shy a quality or two;
but what they wrote is indefensible,
their slights intractable and cruel.
That's my story, and I'm sticking with it.
And I've got a lawyer. And he's vicious too.
"Justice in the extreme is often unjust,"
he said. And at these prices I believe him.

The Moon, It Beckons

Someone said the fields were blue
where the moon had gone to ground.
Someone with drink on their breath
said the fields outside of town
were whited over in early frost.
We few went out to hear the stars complain
about their order and their magnitude.
We passed a last cigarette around,
our talk punctuated by laughter,
our breaths like webbing in the moonset.
Someone said something that stopped us dead,
each of us lost in our own thoughts awhile.
Only then we heard the rippling creekwater
and the cry of the high night overhead.

Magnificent Desolation

Luna. Moon-faced. Moony-eyed.
It's backside mooning the terrible dark.
Dappled with manmade debris
glinting in second-hand sunlight.
So many different shades of grey!
And the way the tides lean toward it,
as if trying to make out every word,
the cosmic hush really rather noisy.

The different faces and phases of the moon.
Like a scythe. Like a star and crescent.
A blue cheesecake with a bite out of it . . .
But I've gone a simile too far,
the moon merely waxing and waning,
tugging the waters, tugging the blood.

Stars At Noon

If you close your eyes
you can see them,
thousands of tiny lighthouses,
a nation of eyes
looking for a needle,
each one suspended
from an angel's hair,
lynched by an angry mob
of plain daylight
for being beautiful,
too unspeakably distant,
too aloof
to be put into words,
into so many words . . .

Cosmological

A lecture about the universe
entitled: By providence or by
design? The static state vs. big
bang theory. As a subset for
the multiverse. The expansion
and the contraction of. Why it
arose from nowt, created, say,
thorium and samarium. How
we extrapolate backwards to
the first millisecond, follow
the causal chain, then that's
that, a cosmic shrug, a shake
of the interstellar head. And
how to make a graceful exit.

As Is

The cosmos set in motion
by a hidden hand,
the world-top wobbling,
an imperceptible bob,
but on a true course,
everything in its place . . .

Sometime during the night
that same hand woke me:
You are older and older . . .
And even darkness dimmed,
its hood over my head,
its game The Terrors.
All to plan, the darkness said.
And no star altered

Shopping After Dark

She needs a cloth of shadows
for patching up the soul's rips.
She orders a measure of dusk
with a pinch of salt for irony.
She buys a roll of evening light
to replace her twitching curtains.
In a twenty-four hour shop
she purchases twenty-four hours
and has it gift-wrapped tout suite.
"A kilo of your finest vitriol,"
she says to the sleepy shopkeeper,
"And put some spit into it."
He toys with the imbalanced scales,
weighing out an ounce of thumb.

The Stations Of The Moth

Where were you when the lights went out?
On the broken shores of sleep, a little fish,
the sea like cold jam, up to my thighs in it.

And the night? An inexplicable bruise,
the trip-wire night to the trapdoor years,
the old coin of moon down, the dark spiraling,
a pharaoh's curse, like the blood of the lamb.

Your dreams? At each breath we lose a number,
some to salt, to war, to ruin;
their quiet sweep through the walls and water.
As if? As if a body in the bed.

And, like any path, a dream just ends —
I awoke to a Big Door slamming, the sky
flushed with acid-orange, the ants roaring.

The Pismire Says

Magnified we're monstrous.
Put us on a page
and we would be lettering,
the words moving, an overly long
sentence striking out in a line.

Cover us in chocolate.
Aren't we quite delectable?
Crunch, we cry loud, crunch.
We taste like chicken.

And out of the hen's eye-hole
climbs the Lord of all the Ants.
He surveys the apocalypse.
"Brothers and sisters of the under-
earth, we have work aplenty."

Salt In The Blood

A glass of water. But the boy
sees thunderheads and wisps
of cloud cover in the Andes. He
says, "All the rivers in the world
end here," and dives from the
perilous cliffs, the sea sucking
in, breathing out. A tumbler
of water, and lightning flashes
across the roof of his mouth, a
storm waging war in the tropics
of his fever. "This is where the
oceans are," he says, the glass
of water too cold to swallow,
waves barging in, weeping out.

Underwater Living

Cold light, waters of the anonymous . . .
How do you tell a stranger you are drowning?
It's a rare fish not fascinated by the silvery lure that's
glinting like a passing conversation or abandoned aqualung,
a semaphore of air bubbles, voices popping to the surface,
agreed upon hand signals at these temperatures and pressure.
Underwater is a bad place for cross purposes —
bodies drift or sink, flounder, know cod philosophies,
wave frantically through the porthole of a sunken trawler,
their spectacles and porcelain perfectly preserved:
but the bones, all that's organic, fed to the fishes. "In school
today we read of pirate treasure, drunken sailors on the rocks,
hopes dashed like ships to kindling." No one mentioned private
wrecks, the awful wrench known as the bends.

The Garden Party

Horticulture's anarchic fringe.
They receive little good press
if they get any press at all: The
mad-eyed gardeners torturing
leaves, pulling out roots like nails,
forming a government of orchids.
"Up with Weeds!" they cried, during
the Allotment Riots. Then "Down
with Rain! Equal rights for lilies!"
they chanted, trampling down the
White House lawn, their thumbs
green, the rose not a rose at all.
A return to Flower Power they
protested, their poor backs aching.

Shrinking Violet

We have no belly for this kind of thing,
our hearts are white, we've the guts of kittens.
A hard wind blows from the mouths of babes,
even the messenger saying nothing, cowering
on the low steps of an unattended temple,
in floodwaters of apathy
fed one urinous drop at a time.

Witness the removal of an apparent spine.
Strike a blow toward a bumptious rib.
Kick another hole in what purports to be a man.
This fever either kills or cures you.
The human rainbow, it requires rain,
it needs the sunlight tearing through us.
Death, it doesn't touch me now. Nor living.

Shrunk

There are signs of the gigantic.
I can barely reach the handles.
A pea takes on dimensions of the sun.
A mere crumb is astronomical.
I put my small back into shifting
an enormous grain of sand.
And it's very cold down here —
apparel loosens, atoms mingle;
molecules are the size of baseballs.
I orbit a planet of dust;
smaller smaller smaller . . .
I'm somewhere between here
and there. I seem to be
then vanish.

Pinpoint

The point was infinitely small.
It expanded, to the size of a dot,
like the one at the end of this sentence.
The immediate area surrounding the dot
was somewhat larger than dot-sized;
albeit smaller than the space
which encompassed that space.
"The way the Universe expanded,"
said the absent-minded physicist,
"from the tiniest pinpoint,"
his place in the cosmos assured.
Which was represented by
an arithmetical progression;
of which zero was the unknown factor.

Gift List

To the novitiate and drunkard —
jazzy checkered slacks and art nouveau.
To the sad-eyed tragedians —
a fascinating aperture, an annihilating hum.
For my suggestible young sister —
the remains of my invisible estate,
the very dishtowel of my displeasure.
To the Society for the Emotionally Disinclined
I'll give candied oranges, Turkish honey,
the last but one of chocolate kisses.
For the one-trick pony president,
addict, starlet, crooner, mug —
the light of winter wrung like mops;
this night, this drink, this moony racket.

She Who Must Be Obeyed

She had a mouth on her like a bee's
bum. She had a voice like a lump of
coal caught under the cellar door. Her
lips parted like the Red Sea when she
said, "I can do anything I want but
I just don't want to." I didn't know
whether to shit or go blind. I whistled
and mopped my forehead with a rag.
The sun dragged its heels across the
sky. And just then, or thereabouts, she
shouted. The birds fell from the trees
like leaves. An ibis died beside the
Nile. Honey blackened in the hive.
And a fish crawled from the water.

Joker

Can't make a shoe, start
a clock, build a house.
Can't save a motor, shape
a drug, attend to wires,
sew trousers, grow turnips,
get a light to go on.

I do mostly useless stuff,
repetitive and thankless tasks
in exchange for a dole;
or bore myself to silliness
with poems and songs,
a sixth sense of humor
rat-rhyming spilt with splat,
then making light of The Fall.

War Song

The West Land is terrible. I go toward this fearful land. I
have come to step over your soul. Your spittle I have put
to rest under the earth. I have come to cover you over in
black rocks, black cloths, black slabs, never to reappear.
Toward the black coffin of the Darkening Land your paths
shall stretch out. So shall it be for you, now that your soul
has faded away. It has become blue. When the darkness
comes your spirit shall grow less and dwindle. Quickly,
this soul shall be without motion. There, under the earth,
where the black war clubs move about like ball sticks in
the game, there your soul shall never reappear. I cause it to
be so. You shall never go and lift up your war club. There,
under the earth, the black war club and the black fog come
together. The black fog shall never be lifted.

Variation of a translation by James Mooney

Pen To Paper

A circle-jerk of historical names —
Stalin, Churchill, Roosevelt —
divvying up the Baltic pie,
the three stooges, out of necessity,
together on the same momentous stage
and about to exercise their penmanship
après le deluge, the shell-shocked
gun-shy ex-soldiers slurrying home
to be de-mobbed back into civvies,
a book for signatures spread-eagled,
blank as Franklin's expression,
Winston pugnacious, Uncle Joe
quasi-smirking, the pen delicately
balanced, like many things, over a page.

A Windless Journey To D

A poem about a man trampled
by starlight, his ropes creaking.
The man as a red berry crushed
between god-teeth, a blood-fat flea,
his bones carved into dice, man-guts
fluttering like flowery ribbons, the
Black Lord's soul-clamps straining
to be purposeful, flesh creeping as
they opened up his skull that night,
the hard-as-diamond cranium, with
a titanium-coated handsaw. Do you
know that taste, our disappointment?
Here I am, the man insists,
more of a threat than an answer.

Cum Laude

The University of Self-perpetuating
Self-myth. As seen on TV. Students
large it up in front of oversized and
multiple mirrors. They're majoring
in ambition, their lectures and lessons
unattended. The headcount lasts all
semester long. Roll calls go on forever.
The Dean networks with a phalanx of
agents, publicists, and very personal
assistants. Big lights cast big shadows,
give off more heat than light, illuminate
the constant bullroar. The graduates go
on to work in me-me-media. Their CVs
sexed-up, legendary, ghost-written.

Hush-A-Bye

The sudden quiet between two voices,
a willow arguing the wind,
the world with the hole in its side,
bad waters urged into the sea —
but mostly silence, sound failing
to travel, to reach the ringing ear,
to cross the spaces expanding
like the parting of two sorrows.

One sense destroyed and four to go.
I went into a land that wasn't listening,
I touched your lips with my cold finger.
These, these are the rare moments
I measure, the what-ifs and what-isn'ts,
the leap to execution from a plan.

Funnybones

Maxims, axioms, old saws and creeds.
Coin of the newspaper press.
The mouth to mouth of a common tongue.
A turn of phrase in the battery of language.
An editor complaining 'a few clichés sneaking in',
which is a cliché in itself, like cock and bull,
genes and memes, and waking up in the morning.

And one I've just seen in a fresh paint,
that I keep worrying as if a chipped tooth,
'tickled to death', the imagery fascinating,
of a death squad itching to get their hands on you,
the jealous lover being kind to be cruel,
a condemned man laughing all the way to the grave,
Death's scythe replaced with a feather.

Out Of Necessity

The Great Inventor has been tinkering
with a bigger bang for your buck
bomb in the basement.
Among his other notable inventions:
thalidomide, napalm, DDT,
the radioactive clock face;
and my old favorite, the siege engine.

This is one who's made the fish
change sex, go belly-up, cry mercury.
And, he's created the self-inflicted wound
that self-infects, the world's tiniest
death ray, and a variety of viruses.
Quiet! Up there in the peanut gallery —
he's about to re-invent the gene.

Unmissable

A film about an empty room, and not
much happening. This includes light
passing through each morning, some
dust, with a mouse's busy footprints,
a fairly peckish spider growing thin
while tending its untested net. A film
that goes on and on for what seems
like centuries, involving a closed door,
a curtain moving by a window, rain
tapping at the glass, the dark nights,
floorboards creaking mysteriously.
"Thumbs up!" say the critics. "Four stars!"
They especially loved the fly guest-
starring, and the inevitably sad ending.

Fame Is A Fly

All my scenes left on the cutting-
room floor, as if I'd never existed.
Me, singing in the rain, phoning home;
me, screaming in the shower. A star
of stage and screen reduced to sweepings,
washed-up, a legend of boffo box-office
left off the director's cut. Cursed fame
is a one-eyed Gila monster masquerading
as a dinosaur. Fame is a double, a stand-
in, a back lot extra, a stuntman who was
injured in a fall. Just imagine, ME, a star
with stardust in his eyes, the ability
to weep and laugh on cue. My best
lines overdubbed by Italian actors.

On The Town

A nightclub called the Comfort
Zone. You saw me fleeing with
an incendiary blonde on one arm
and an imaginary brunette on the
other, leaving that sea of booze
and jazz behind, a cheeky wink
into the cameras of the waiting
paparazzi. The taxi driver, the
seventh son of a seventh son,
pawed at the steering wheel
violently as we pulled out into
traffic. You saw a rose, clenched
between his teeth, the wandering
star he used to guide us.

Risen

It rises from the cookie jar, out of the mouse's ear.
It rises from a cold black cup of coffee.
It rises from a drain, an eyeless worm,
an ocean fog, a deadly vapor, the vipers' breaths.
It rises like the sunrise over Titan,
like a blood-drenched flag in mustard gas,
a balloon the children let go at the fair.
It rises from the ashtray, from a grey discarded slipper.
It rises, like the baby's caterwaul,
from its bed of nails, from a cold tomb on the third day.
As if dust-devils, as if a cobra, like Orion;
up and up and up it rose, cradled on a burdened wind:
That thing that doesn't have a name,
and no one, and no thing, can stop it.

Three Ring Circus

Bring on the juggling dogs
and their glamorous assistant.
Introducing Mr. Solar Plexus,
and his incredible dancing
bread-basket. Come one, come
all; see the death-defying death-
defiers defying death: For three
nights only. And Biff and Boff,
two clowns bathed in pathos
and beating the lights out of one
another; just for the hell of it.
And without a net, a fish on the
flying trapeze. And under the
Big Top, some singing horses.

Nursery Crimes

Old Mother Hubbard went to the
filing cabinet and studied your
details closely. She lived in a shoe
box. She gave her old man a loan.
She had so many children she couldn't
feed them. Little Jack Horner sat in the
witness stand. He pulled out a gun. He
stuck out his tongue, said, "What a good
lawyer have I." Jack be nimble, Jack B.
Quick, Jack nicked your silver candlesticks.
Simple Simon met a high man heading
for despair. Jack and Jill went up before
the magistrate. No one lived happily ever
after. And Mary had a little problem . . .

In Cartoonland

Eyes bulge from balloon-like heads
that pop at the point of a pin.
A crow in black-face saws a branch
but the tree falls down, with him in it.
A dog and a pig and a duck in a bed;
and all the cars have smiling faces.
Just listen to those sound effects:
sprong and splat and boink and gong.
And the typically unsuitable music;
brooms singing, a finger missing,
characters half animal, half man —
with hats on, but buck-naked,
who live through explosions and fire —
suddenly bursting into flame or song.

Leave It Out

A fleet of sleek silver people-carriers
snaked through the streets. Night-
choppers hovered noisily as alarms
rang, ignored. There were distractions —
five years of research wasted. A cop
gave me the Evil Eye from which I never
fully recovered. It was unseasonably cool,

which has little bearing on the matter,
but I thought that I should mention
it. This is the harsh reality of which
we have little choice but to confront:
it's difficult to know what to leave in or
out. I have included the completed form,
and an unsatisfactory sky, bullet-colored.

One Minus One Is None

Not in the making of the snowman,
but its destruction.
Not its construction,
nor its creation;
neither the sound of the children
nor a foothold gained —
but the warmth, and the wind, and the rain.

Half a sonnet is better than none.
Two are twice as good as one.
It's not in the winning
of the race begun,
and it's not the legend of the sun —
this is the beginning —
and the thing is done.

Acknowledgements

Many of these poems first appeared in the following journals: *Mused (BellaOnline), 14, Coe Review, The Dawn Treader, Earth's Daughter, The Journal (U.K.), Decanto, Poetic Hours, Pulsar, The Interpreter's House, The Prairie Journal, Fire, Labour of Love, Moonstone, The View From Here, Island Writer, Verse Wisconsin, Ozone Park Journal* and *Markings.*

Bio

Bruce McRae, a Canadian musician, came to poetry late but has enjoyed a large number of publications in the past 10 years, recently gaining airplay for his poems and songs in the U.K., Australia and the U.S.A. *The So-called Sonnets* is his first book. More information can be found on his website: www.bpmcrae.com.